HEAL, GROW, COACH

BY DR. TANDY NANCE

ABOUT THE AUTHOR

As the Founder and CEO of Redesign Your Life, LLC. Dr.Tandy Nance is a highly accomplished and dedicated Metaphysician, Certified Holistic Life Coach, International Author, and motivational Speaker. With over 18 years of experience in the mental health field, Dr. Tandy has amassed an impressive array of academic qualifications, including a Bachelor's degree in Criminal Justice, a Master's degree in Counseling Studies, a Master's degree in Business Administration, and a Doctorate in Metaphysical Humanistic Science.

Dr. Tandy is also the self-published author of "The Diva Code," a guide to leveling up designed to encourage self-improvement; the motivational self-help book "Boundaries+Clarity=Peace," which is designed to assist individuals who are struggling to create boundaries and gain the clarity necessary to make positive changes in their lives; "Your Body Is Your Castle," a six-week guide to eating healthier and having a positive body image; and co-author of "Forgiveness Is Therapeutic," created to emphasize the power of forgiveness, healing, and moving forward. She is also the author of "Date Thyself," a book focused on breaking the cycle of toxic relationships and changing one's energy signature to attract different people into one's life, and "Heal, Grow, Coach," a guide that offers insights and strategies for personal growth and becoming an effective coach. Her books aim to empower people to find peace and fulfillment in their lives.

Copyright Page

Copyright © 2023 Dr. Tandy Nance

Dedication

I dedicate this book to all the past and future coaches who started their journey with Redesign Your Life, LLC. Heal, Grow, Coach!

-Dr. Tandy

INTRODUCTION

Alright, let's get one thing straight: healing is not a walk in the park. It's more like a trek through the wilderness with no map, no compass, and a backpack full of emotional baggage. And guess what? That's okay! Because here's the truth: the path to becoming a life coach, a real coach, starts with healing yourself first. You can't guide someone out of their mess if you're still tangled up in yours.

So, welcome to "Heal, Grow, Coach"—your new best friend on this wild ride. This isn't just another self-help book; this is a call to action. It's time to put on your big-girl (or big-boy) pants and face those skeletons in the closet. The only way out is through, my friend, and this book is here to help you navigate the journey from wounded to warrior, from healer to guide.

UNDERSTANDING THE JOURNEY OF HEALING AND GROWTH

Now, here's where the magic happens. Once you've done the hard work of healing, you don't just sit there, patting yourself on the back. Oh no, honey bun. You take that newfound strength, that clarity, and that wisdom, and you use it to help others. Because that's what a life coach does—we guide, we inspire, we kick a little butt when necessary (with love, of course).

A real-life coach knows what it's like to be at rock bottom. We understand the struggle, the tears, the frustration of not knowing which way is up. And that's why we're so damn good at what we do. We don't just talk the talk; we've walked the walk. We've climbed out of our pits, and now we're reaching back with a hand to help others do the same. It's not just a job; it's a calling. And trust me, once you start, there's no going back.

WHY THIS BOOK?

So, why this book? Why should you trust me to guide you on this journey? Because I've been there, done that, and got the scars to prove it. I've faced my demons, I've wrestled with my fears, and I've come out the other side stronger and more determined than ever. I know what it's like to feel lost, to wonder if things will ever get better. And I also know the incredible joy of finding my way, of healing, of growing, and of stepping into the role of a coach—a boss, a mentor, a healer.

This book is for you if you're ready to stop playing small and start living large. If you're tired of the same old patterns and ready for a breakthrough. If you want to heal, grow, and then take that growth and turn it into a force for good in the world. I'm here to show you how to do it, step by step, with a little sass, a lot of heart, and all the tools you'll need to redesign your life and the lives of others.

So, buckle up, buttercup. It's time to heal, to grow, and to become the coach you were always meant to be. Let's get to work!

Dr. Tandy

PART 1

Healing

CHAPTER 1
Understanding Your Wounds

Alright, let's dive in. If you're here to become a life coach, first things first—you've got to do some serious self-work. You can't just slap a band-aid on your old wounds and call it a day. Oh no, honey bun! You need to roll up your sleeves, dig deep, and face those skeletons in the closet. Trust me, your clients will thank you later.

"Self-work is the greatest gift you can give yourself. It's the foundation for growth, the catalyst for change, and the pathway to becoming the best version of you. When you do the inner work, the world around you shifts.
-Dr. Tandy

IDENTIFYING PERSONAL TRAUMAS AND UNRESOLVED ISSUES

Let's talk about trauma for a second. Trauma isn't just the big stuff—like losing someone you love or surviving a natural disaster. It can also be those sneaky little things that nibble away at your self-worth over time, like that one mean teacher who told you you'd never amount to anything, or the heartbreak from that first love who ghosted you. Yep, those count too!

To heal, you've got to identify these personal traumas and unresolved issues. Dig up those roots, baby, because if you don't, they'll keep sprouting weeds in your life. You know that feeling when something triggers you and you suddenly react in a way that even surprises you? That's the ghost of traumas past knocking on your door.

Start by asking yourself, what's still haunting me? Be brutally honest. What's that one memory that still makes your stomach churn or that fear that keeps you playing small? Write them down, get them out of your head, and onto paper where you can face them.

THE IMPORTANCE OF ACKNOWLEDGING YOUR OWN PAIN BEFORE HELPING OTHERS

Listen up, because this is where most wannabe coaches get it twisted: You cannot, I repeat, cannot help others if you haven't helped yourself first. It's like trying to pour from an empty cup—nothing's gonna come out except maybe some hot air and frustration.

Acknowledging your own pain isn't a sign of weakness; it's a badge of honor. It means you're brave enough to face the truth, no matter how ugly it might be. And let me tell you, facing your pain is the only way to heal from it. When you've done your own work, you'll be able to recognize those signs in others. You'll be able to say, "I've been there. I get it. And I know how to help you climb out of this pit."

Think of it like this, would you trust a fitness coach who's never been to the gym? No way! The same goes for life coaching. If you've never dealt with your own pain, how are you supposed to guide someone else through theirs?

EXERCISES FOR SELF-REFLECTION AND JOURNALING

Now, you know we can't just talk about healing—we've got to do the work. So grab your journal, because it's time for some self-reflection exercises. Don't roll your eyes at me; this is where the magic happens!

1.The Trigger Tracker: For the next week, I want you to jot down every time something or someone triggers an intense emotional reaction in you. What happened? How did it make you feel? What's the earliest memory you have of feeling this way? This exercise helps you connect the dots between past wounds and present reactions.

2.Letter to Your Younger Self: Write a letter to the younger you. Tell them what you know now that you wish you'd known then. Acknowledge their pain, their struggles, and offer them the comfort they needed back then. This exercise is powerful for healing old wounds and finding closure.

3.Mirror Work: Stand in front of a mirror, look yourself in the eyes, and speak your truths. Say out loud the things you've been afraid to admit, even to yourself. Then, forgive yourself for holding onto them for so long. It's going to feel weird, maybe even a bit awkward, but keep going. The mirror doesn't lie, and neither should you.

These exercises are just the beginning. Healing is a process—a messy, beautiful, transformational process. You've got to commit to it like you're committing to a lifelong love affair with yourself. Remember, you're doing this not just for you, but for every client you're going to help down the line. So, let's heal those wounds and turn them into wisdom. You've got this!

CHAPTER 2

The Healing Process

Alright, beautiful souls, it's time to roll up those sleeves and get into the nitty-gritty of healing. Now, healing isn't a one-size-fits-all deal. Just like you wouldn't wear the same outfit to a beach party and a boardroom meeting (unless you're into making bold statements), you need different tools for different wounds. So, let's explore the wonderful world of healing modalities, find what works for you, and start stitching up those battle scars.

"The healing process is not about erasing the pain, but about transformin it into wisdom. It's a journey of self-discovery, where every wound becomes a lesson, and every scar a testament to your strength."
-DR. TANDY

EXPLORING VARIOUS HEALING MODALITIES

Let's be real, healing is like an all-you-can-eat buffet. You've got to try a little bit of everything to see what nourishes your soul. Some of you might need a big ol' serving of mindfulness, while others might be reaching for a heaping plate of energy healing. And hey, don't knock it 'til you try it! Here's a taste of what's on the menu:

- **Energy Healing:** Let's talk about energy, honey. It's everywhere. It's in the air, it's in your body, and sometimes, it's all blocked up like traffic at rush hour. That's where energy healing comes in to save the day! Techniques like the Emotion Code and Hypnotherapy are all about getting that energy flowing smoothly again. Think of it as a spiritual tune-up for your soul's engine. You may not see those energetic kinks, but oh, you'll definitely feel the difference when they get worked out.

And guess what? I'm certified in both of these powerful modalities, so if you're feeling stuck or blocked, it might be time to reach out to me. Together, we can clear out those energy roadblocks and get you moving forward on your path to healing and transformation.

- **Mindfulness:** Mindfulness isn't just a buzzword; it's a way of life. It's about being present, in the moment, and truly feeling your feelings without letting them drive the bus. It's about catching yourself before you fall down the rabbit hole of anxiety or past regrets. Being mindful allows you to slow down, take a breath, and respond to life's curveballs with grace instead of panic.
- **Meditation:** If you think meditation is all about sitting cross-legged and chanting "om," think again! Meditation is your daily mental shower, washing off all the stress and grime that accumulates. Whether you're visualizing your happy place, focusing on your breath, or using guided meditations, this practice helps you clear the mental clutter and tune into your inner wisdom.

And that's just the start! There's also journaling, yoga, sound healing, breathwork, and a whole host of other tools that can help you on your journey. The key is to find what resonates with you and to be open to trying new things. Remember, healing is a deeply personal journey, and there's no wrong way to do it as long as it's helping you grow.

HOW TO CREATE A PERSONAL HEALING PLAN

Alright, now that we've laid out the buffet, it's time to make your plate. Creating a personal healing plan isn't about cramming every single modality into your life at once. (We're healing here, not overstuffing ourselves at Thanksgiving!) It's about finding what works for you and making it a consistent part of your life.

Here's how to whip up your personal healing recipe:

1. **Access Your Needs:** Take a good, hard look at where you're at right now. What are you struggling with the most? Anxiety? Self-doubt? Anger? Figure out what you need to focus on first. It's like Marie Kondo-ing your life—what needs the most attention right now?

2. **Choose Your Modalities:** Based on your needs, choose a couple of healing modalities to start with. If you're feeling disconnected from yourself, maybe start with mindfulness and meditation. If you're holding onto a lot of past pain, energy healing might be your ticket. And remember, it's okay to mix and match. Healing isn't linear—it's a dance, and you're leading!

3. **Set Realistic Goals:** We're not going for perfection here; we're going for progress. Set small, achievable goals for yourself. Maybe it's meditating for five minutes each morning or practicing mindfulness during your lunch break. Whatever it is, make sure it's something you can commit to without feeling overwhelmed.

4. **Create a Routine:** Healing happens in the everyday moments, not just the big, breakthrough ones. Incorporate your chosen modalities into your daily routine. Remember, this is about consistency, not intensity. You don't have to be perfect; you just have to show up.

5. **Reflect and Adjust:** Check in with yourself regularly. What's working? What isn't? Be flexible and willing to switch things up if something doesn't feel right. Healing is an ongoing process, not a destination. Keep tweaking your plan as you go along, and don't be afraid to try new things.

Now, let me tell you something about resilience. It's not just about bouncing back; it's about bouncing forward. It's about taking those hard knocks, dusting yourself off, and saying, "Is that all you've got?" Let me introduce you to some real-life warriors who've done just that, and trust me, their stories are going to light a fire under you.

Take Maya, for example. She came to me with a heart full of hurt from a toxic relationship that had her questioning her worth. We started with a combination of **meditation, Emotion Code,** and my **Date ThySelf** program, that's when the magic began. She dug deep into those old wounds, releasing all the emotional baggage that had been weighing her down for years. Slowly but surely, she started to see herself not as a victim, but as a survivor. Today, Maya is a beacon of strength and self-love, using her own journey to help others heal their hearts.

Then there's Jamal, who had been carrying around a lifetime of anger from a childhood where he never felt like he was enough. Through **Emotion Code, and hypnotherapy**, Jamal learned how to release that pent-up rage, letting it go like an exhale he'd been holding in for years. Once we cleared those energetic blocks, he transformed that anger into passion, becoming a motivational speaker who now helps others turn their pain into power. Talk about a comeback story!

These aren't just stories—they're proof of what happens when you commit to your healing. Whether it's through Emotion Code, hypnotherapy, or any other powerful modality, there's a way out of that stuck, heavy feeling. And, honey bun, I'm certified in these techniques, so if you need some help getting started, reach out to me. Together, we can turn those wounds into wisdom.

So, let's get to work! Healing isn't a destination—it's a journey. And every single step you take is a step toward the powerful, unstoppable person you're meant to become. Ready? Let's do this!

CHAPTER 3
Building Emotional Resilience

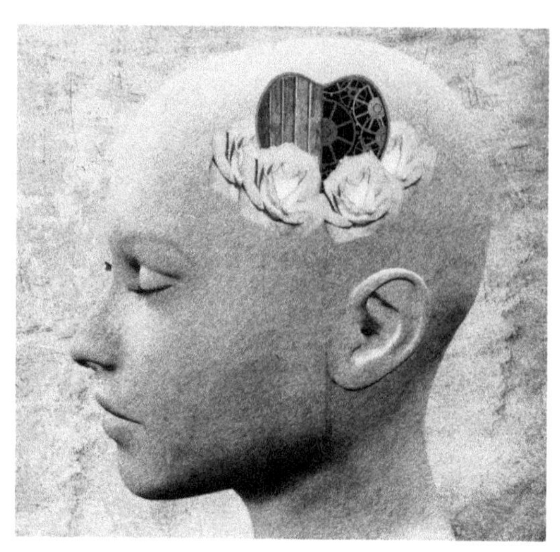

Let's get one thing straight, emotional resilience isn't just about surviving the storms—it's about dancing in the rain. Life is going to throw some serious curveballs your way, and the key to staying strong is learning how to catch them without falling apart. Emotional resilience is your superpower, and guess what? It's not something you're born with—it's something you build. So, let's talk about how to become the emotional powerhouse you're meant to be.

DEVELOPING EMOTIONAL INTELLIGENCE AND RESILIENCE

First things first, emotional resilience and emotional intelligence are two sides of the same coin. You can't have one without the other. Emotional intelligence is all about being aware of your own emotions, understanding them, and knowing how to respond to them in a healthy way. It's also about tuning into the emotions of others and responding with empathy, rather than with knee-jerk reactions.

Now, emotional resilience kicks in when things go sideways. It's the ability to keep your cool, process your feelings, and bounce forward (not just back!) when life gets tough. Think of emotional resilience as your emotional muscle—it gets stronger the more you work on it. And the best part? Anyone can develop it. Yes, that includes you.

Here's how you start building emotional resilience:

1. **Self-awareness:** Pay attention to your emotions. Notice when you're feeling stressed, anxious, or triggered. The more aware you are, the quicker you can address what's going on before it spirals out of control.

2. **Emotional Regulation:** Learn how to manage your emotions instead of letting them manage you. When you feel overwhelmed, take a pause. Breathe. Give yourself space to process before reacting.

3. **Empathy**: Developing emotional intelligence isn't just about you. It's about understanding the emotions of others too. When you can empathize with people, you respond to situations with grace instead of frustration.

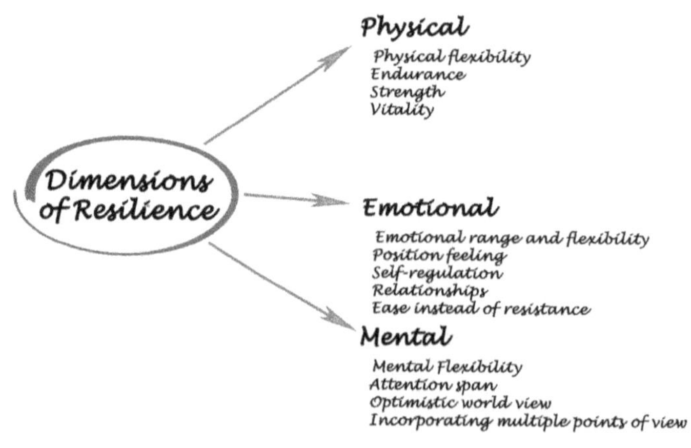

TECHNIQUES FOR MANAGING STRESS, ANXIETY, AND EMOTIONAL TRIGGERS

Life can be like walking through a minefield of stress and emotional triggers—one wrong step, and BOOM. But here's the good news: you don't have to walk around on edge all the time. There are techniques you can use to diffuse those emotional bombs and manage stress like a pro.

1. **Breathwork:** You know that feeling when stress starts to bubble up, and your chest gets tight? That's your body telling you it's in fight-or-flight mode. The quickest way to calm yourself down is to breathe. Try this: inhale slowly for 4 counts, hold for 4 counts, exhale for 4 counts. Repeat until you feel your body relax. This technique can literally reset your nervous system.

2. **Grounding Exercises:** When anxiety hits, it can feel like you're spiraling out of control. Grounding exercises help bring you back to the present moment. One simple way is to use your five senses: focus on what you can see, hear, touch, smell, and taste around you. This helps anchor you in the here and now.

4. **Visualization:** Your mind is powerful, so use it! When stress creeps in, close your eyes and visualize a peaceful place—somewhere that makes you feel calm and safe. Imagine yourself there, breathing in that calm energy. Visualization tricks your brain into relaxing, even when you're under pressure.

5. **Journaling:** If your emotions are all over the place, write it out. Journaling helps you process your feelings and get them out of your head and onto paper. Plus, when you look back, you'll start to notice patterns—what triggers you, what helps you cope—and that self-awareness is golden.

6. **Mindful Movement:** Stress and anxiety get stuck in your body, so get moving! Whether it's yoga, walking, or dancing around your living room, moving your body helps release tension and stress. It also gives your mind a break from overthinking.

7. **Set Boundaries:** Sometimes, managing stress is about knowing when to say "no." If you're constantly stretched thin, you're going to burn out. Protect your energy by setting boundaries with people and situations that drain you.

BUILDING A SUPPORT SYSTEM FOR YOUR HEALING JOURNEY

Let me be clear. you don't have to go through this alone. Building emotional resilience doesn't mean you have to be an island. In fact, one of the most powerful ways to stay strong is by surrounding yourself with the right people. A solid support system is like having a personal emotional safety net—it catches you when you fall and lifts you when you're ready to rise again.

Here's how you can build your emotional dream team:

1. **Identify Your Inner Circle**: These are your ride-or-die people—the ones who support you unconditionally, who lift you up when you're down, and who tell you the truth when you need to hear it (even if it's hard). Your inner circle should consist of people who understand your journey, respect your boundaries, and encourage your growth.

2. **Seek Professional Support:** Sometimes, friends and family aren't enough—and that's okay! There's no shame in reaching out to a therapist, coach, or counselor. Having a professional who can guide you through your healing process can be life-changing. If you're feeling stuck or overwhelmed, don't hesitate to get that extra support.

3. **Find Like-Minded Communities:** Whether it's a support group, an online community, or a wellness circle, finding people who are on a similar journey can be incredibly empowering. You'll not only receive support, but you'll also be reminded that you're not alone in this process. We all need a tribe, so don't be afraid to find yours.

4. **Practice Vulnerability:** Emotional resilience doesn't mean shutting people out; it means knowing when to let them in. Practice being vulnerable with the people you trust. Share your struggles, ask for help, and be open to receiving support. Vulnerability is a strength, not a weakness.

Conclusion

Building emotional resilience is about more than just toughing it out—it's about growing through what you go through. It's about becoming emotionally intelligent, learning how to manage stress and anxiety, and creating a solid support system to catch you when life gets hard. With these tools in your emotional toolkit, you'll be able to handle whatever life throws your way with grace and grit.

So, let's get started. You've got this. Let's build that emotional muscle and start dancing through the storms. Because honey bun, you're stronger than you know.

PART 2
Grow

CHAPTER 4

The Growth Mindset

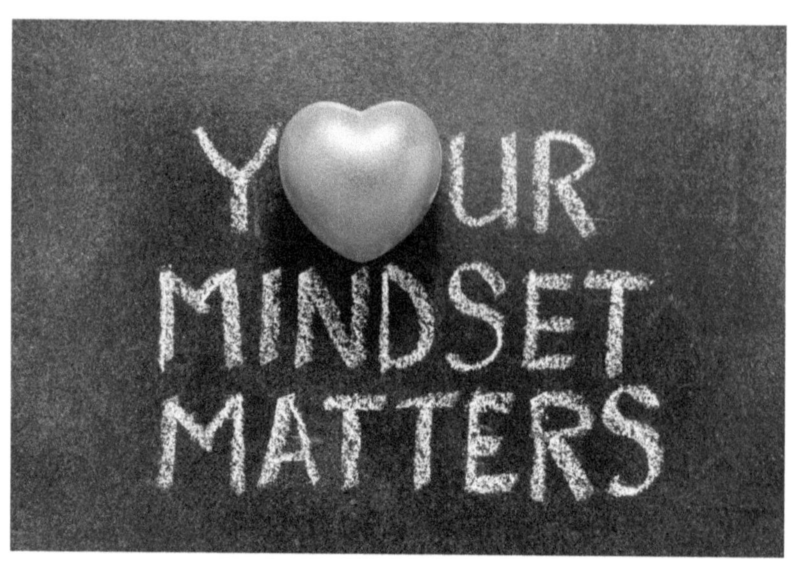

Alright, let's get into it—the Growth Mindset. Now, before we dive in, let me ask you something: Are you stuck in your own head, believing that what you've got is all there is? Or are you ready to embrace the idea that you're capable of leveling up in ways you never thought possible? If you answered yes to the latter, you're in the right place. If you're still hanging out in the "I'm not enough" zone, don't worry, I've got you covered.

"Growth begins when you stop seeing challenges as obstacles and start viewing them as opportunities. A growth mindset transforms limitations into limitless possibilities."
-DR. TANDY

UNDERSTANDING THE DIFFERENCE BETWEEN A FIXED MINDSET AND A GROWTH MINDSET

Let me break it down for you. A fixed mindset is like living in a house with no windows. You're stuck inside, looking at the same old four walls. thinking, "Well, this is it." You believe your abilities are set in stone, and you avoid challenges because, deep down, you don't think you can handle them. You might even think. "Why bother trying if I'm going to fail anyway?"

Sound familiar? Yeah, that's the fixed mindset talking, and it's time to shut that voice down.

Now, a growth mindset, on the other hand, is like flinging open the windows of that house and realizing there's a whole world outside. It's believing that you can learn, grow, and improve—no matter what life throws at you. When you've got a growth mindset, you're not afraid to fail because you know that failure isn't the end of the road; it's just a pit stop on the way to success.

Let me hit you with some science real quick: people with a growth mindset believe that their talents and intelligence can be developed through hard work, learning, and persistence. That's a game-changer, baby, because once you get that down, nothing can stop you. Challenges? You eat those for breakfast. Criticism? You take it and run with it. Setbacks? Honey, those are just stepping stones to the next level.

RATEGIES TO CULTIVATE A GROWTH MINDSET IN YOUR PERSONAL AND PROFESSIONAL LIFE

So, how do you shift from a fixed mindset to a growth mindset? Let me tell you, it's not some magical overnight transformation where you wake up one morning and suddenly you're all about personal development. Nope. It takes intention, but it's so worth it.

Here are a few ways to start flexing those growth mindset muscles:

1. **Embrace Challenges:** Look, nobody likes to struggle, but growth happens when you step out of your comfort zone. The next time you face a challenge, instead of running for the hills, ask yourself, "What can I learn from this?" Get curious! Challenges are opportunities in disguise, so lean into them.

2. **Reframe Failure**: I know, failing sucks. But here's the thing—you only fail when you stop trying. If something doesn't work out, don't call it a failure; call it feedback. Ask yourself, "What didn't go right? What can I do differently next time?" Growth-minded people don't see failure as a roadblock; they see it as a detour on the road to success.

3. **Practice Grit:** Success is about resilience, honey. Grit means sticking with something even when it's hard, even when you're tired, even when you don't see immediate results. It's about putting in the work day after day. In personal and professional life, grit is what separates the talkers from the doers.

4. **Surround Yourself with Growth-Oriented People:** You know the saying, "You are the average of the five people you spend the most time with"? Yeah, that's real. If you want to grow, you need to hang out with people who push you, challenge you, and support your goals. No more keeping yourself small to make others feel comfortable. It's time to level up your circle.

5. **Celebrate Progress, Not Perfection:** Perfection is a myth, but progress? That's real, and it's worth celebrating. Don't wait for the end goal to pat yourself on the back. Acknowledge every step forward, no matter how small. Growth is a journey, and the destination keeps moving—so learn to love the ride.

OVERCOMING SELF-DOUBT AND FEAR OF FAILURE

Let's talk about that nagging little voice in your head —the one that whispers, "You can't do this," or "Who do you think you are?" Yeah, self-doubt is a sneaky little monster, and it loves to show up just when you're about to take a big leap. But here's the deal, self-doubt doesn't have to run the show.

Self-doubt and **fear** of failure are nothing more than old stories you've been telling yourself. They're based on past experiences, other people's opinions, and that fixed mindset we talked about earlier. But guess what? You are the author of your own story, and you can rewrite those tired old scripts.

Here's how to kick self-doubt to the curb:

1. **Call It Out:** When that voice starts whispering negative nonsense in your ear, don't just let it ramble on. Recognize it for what it is—fear. Say, "Oh Okay, fear, I see you. But you're not driving today." Acknowledge it and then choose not to believe it.

2. **Focus on the Facts:** Self-doubt is based on feelings, not facts. When you feel that wave of insecurity, remind yourself of what you've already accomplished. Write down your wins—big or small. Build a case for your success, and when self-doubt creeps in, read that list and shut it down.

3. **Flip the Script:** Instead of thinking, "What if I fail?" ask yourself, "What if I succeed?" Don't focus on what could go wrong. Visualize everything going right. Your mind is a powerful tool, and what you focus on, you attract. So start focusing on success, not failure.

4. **Take Imperfect Action:** Here's the secret: nobody feels 100% ready when they start something new. Waiting for the perfect moment or until you "feel ready" is just a recipe for procrastination. Take action, even if it's messy. Every step you take builds confidence, and before you know it, self-doubt won't stand a chance.

5. **Remember Your Why:** When fear tries to talk you out of going after your dreams, remind yourself why you started. Your "why" is your anchor. It's what keeps you going when things get tough. Whether it's your family, your passion, or your mission to make an impact, hold onto that reason and let it drive you forward.

Wrapping It Up

Cultivating a growth mindset isn't about being fearless or never doubting yourself. It's about recognizing that you have the power to grow, learn, and adapt no matter what comes your way. When you make that shift from a fixed mindset to a growth mindset, you'll find yourself overcoming challenges, smashing through self-doubt, and achieving things you once thought were impossible.

So, are you ready to embrace the growth mindset? Are you ready to step into your full potential, knowing that you're capable of more than you've ever imagined? Let's go get it, because the only thing standing between you and your greatness is the belief that you can grow into it.

Now go on, make it happen!

CHAPTER 5
Personal Development Tools

Alright, let's get down to the real talk: personal development tools are the secret sauce to redesigning your life. You didn't think you'd just stumble into greatness without a plan, did you? No, honey bun, success doesn't just happen by accident. It's the result of intentional action, and lucky for you, I'm about to spill all the tea on how to make that happen. We're talking goal-setting, vision boards, affirmations, and my personal favorite—creating habits and routines that will have you thriving like never before.

"Personal development tools are the keys to unlocking your potential. With the right tools, you can shape your life, sharpen your mind, and strengthen your spirit."
-DR. TANDY

GOAL-SETTING: THE ROADMAP TO YOUR SUCCES

Now, before we get into the fancy tools, let me hit you with some truth: if you don't know where you're going, you're going nowhere. Goal-setting is like putting the GPS coordinates into your life's navigation system. Without clear goals, you're just driving in circles, hoping to end up somewhere good. Spoiler alert: that's not how it works!

Here's the Dr. Tandy formula for setting goals that stick:

1. **Be Specific:** None of this "I want to be successful" or "I want to feel better" nonsense. What does success look like to you? What does "feeling better" mean in your day-to-day life? Get crystal clear on what you want. If you can't define it, you can't achieve it.

2. **Make It Measurable:** Goals need to be measurable so you can track your progress. Want to write a book? Great! How many pages or chapters will you write each week? Want to start your own business? Awesome! How many clients or sales do you need to consider it a win?

3. **Set a Deadline**: A goal without a deadline is just a wish. You've got to give yourself a timeline. Saying "someday" isn't going to cut it. If you're serious about leveling up, put a time stamp on those goals and get to work.

4. **Break It Down:** Big goals can feel overwhelming, so break them down into bite-sized, manageable tasks. It's like building a house—you don't just throw up the whole structure in one day. You start with the foundation, then move onto the walls, and before you know it, you're picking out drapes for the windows. Small steps lead to big wins.

VISION BOARDS: SEE IT, BELIEVE IT, ACHIEVE IT

Now let's talk about the power of vision boards. And don't you dare roll your eyes—this is where the magic happens. A vision board is like your personal Pinterest page for success. It's a visual representation of everything you want to achieve, everything you want to become, and everything you want to have. The secret? When you see it, your brain starts to believe it.

Here's how to make your vision board work for you:

1. **Get Creative:** Grab some magazines, print out pictures from online, or even get artsy with it and draw your own images. Include pictures and words that represent your goals, whether that's a dream home, a thriving business, or a sense of peace and happiness.

2. **Place It Where You Can See It:** Put that vision board somewhere you'll see it every single day. This is a reminder of what you're working toward, and it keeps your goals front and center. Every time you look at it, you're reinforcing your intention to make those dreams a reality.

3. **Feel the Energy:** This is key—don't just look at your vision board like it's a pretty picture. Feel the energy of what it would be like to live those goals. Imagine yourself already there. When you embody the feelings of success, happiness, or whatever you're striving for, you start attracting it like a magnet.

AFFIRMATIONS: SPEAK IT INTO EXISTENCE

Let's talk affirmations. Some people think they're cheesy, but those people aren't leveling up like you're about to. Affirmations are powerful statements that remind you of who you are, what you're capable of, and what you're working toward. They shift your mindset from self-doubt to self-belief.

Here's how to slay the affirmation game:

1. **Make Them Positive:** Forget the "I hope" and "I want" language. Your affirmations should be I am choosing to and I have. "I am choosing to be successful." "I have everything I need to achieve my goals." Speak it like it's already true, and watch how your mind starts to align with that truth. By saying "I am choosing to," you're reminding yourself that you are in control of your actions and mindset, and you're making an active decision to embrace the life you want.

2. **Say Them Daily:** Morning, noon, and night—affirmations are like brushing your teeth. You've got to do it regularly if you want to see results. Repeating your affirmations daily helps reprogram your mind and pushes out all that negative self-talk.

3. **Believe It:** Don't just say the words; feel them. If you say, "I am confident," but your inner voice is like, "Yeah, right," keep saying it until that voice quiets down. Eventually, your mind will catch up with your words.

THE POWER OF HABITS AND ROUTINES IN PERSONAL GROWTH

Listen, you can have all the goals, vision boards, and affirmations in the world, but if you don't have habits and routines in place, you're going to struggle to get results. The power of habits is that they take you out of autopilot and put you in the driver's seat of your life. It's about creating daily systems that move you closer to your goals without you even realizing it.

Here's how to master the art of habits and routines:

1. **Start Small**: Rome wasn't built in a day, and neither are successful habits. Start with small changes—wake up 15 minutes earlier, write down three things you're grateful for, or commit to reading 10 pages a day. Once these small habits become second nature, you can stack more onto them.

2. **Consistency Over Intensity:** You don't need to overhaul your whole life in a week. What matters is showing up, day in and day out. Small, consistent actions lead to massive results over time. The key is doing a little bit every day, even when you don't feel like it. Especially when you don't feel like it!

3. **Create a Routine That Works for You:** There's no "right" way to structure your day. Some people are morning people, and others thrive at night. The goal is to create a routine that supports your energy levels and your goals. Whether it's a morning meditation or a late-night writing session, find what works for you and stick to it.

CASE STUDIES: REAL PEOPLE, REAL RESULTS

Let me give you some receipts—because you know I don't just talk the talk.

Case Study #1: Alicia's Confidence Comeback

Alicia came to me struggling with self-doubt. She had big dreams but didn't believe she had what it took to achieve them. We started with daily affirmations, goal-setting, and a vision board. Slowly, as she repeated her affirmations and kept her vision front and center, she started to believe in herself. Within six months, Alicia landed her dream job, built stronger relationships, and most importantly, transformed how she saw herself. She stopped hoping for confidence and started living it.

Case Study #2: Jasmine's Coaching Business Breakthrough

Jasmine was stuck in a corporate job she hated, constantly daydreaming about starting her own coaching business but paralyzed by fear. We worked together on goal-setting and creating habits that would support her vision. She started waking up an hour earlier to focus on building her coaching practice, setting specific goals for launching her services, and kept her vision board front and center. Fast forward a year, and Jasmine now runs a thriving coaching business, working on her own terms and empowering others to live their best lives—just like she once dreamed.

Wrapping It Up

Personal development tools aren't just gimmicks—they're your blueprint for success. Whether it's setting goals, visualizing your dreams, speaking your affirmations, or building habits that support your growth, these tools are designed to get you where you want to go. And trust me, when you put them into action, you'll be unstoppable.

So, let's get to it! Grab your goals, your vision, and your affirmations, and start creating a routine that sets you up for greatness. You've got everything you need to redesign your life—now go make it happen!

CHAPTER 6
Discovering Your Purpose and Passion

Alright, gorgeous souls, let's get into the juicy stuff —purpose and passion. Now, I know what you're thinking: "Dr. Tandy, how am I supposed to find my purpose when I'm just trying to make it through the day?" Well, buckle up, because we're about to dig deep and uncover what lights your soul on fire. Your purpose isn't some mystical thing hidden in a far-off place; it's inside you, and we're going to bring it out into the light.

"Discovering your purpose is like finding your true north—it gives your life direction, meaning, and the power to move forward with intention."
-DR. TANDY

TECHNIQUES FOR FINDING YOUR PURPOSE AND PASSION

Here's the truth, you weren't put on this earth to just clock in, pay bills, and call it a day. You were meant to thrive, to feel alive, and to make an impact. But how do you discover what that impact is supposed to be? Let me hit you with some tools that'll help you figure it out.

1. **Reflect on What Brings You Joy:** Purpose and passion go hand in hand, and the first step to finding them is thinking about what makes you feel alive. What are the activities that make you lose track of time? What are the things that, even when you're tired, you'd still get up and do? If it doesn't make your heart skip a beat, it's not your passion, honey bun.

2. **Look Back at Your Life's Clues:** Your life has been dropping hints about your purpose for a long time. Think back to your childhood—what did you love doing? What came naturally to you? Sometimes, our passions are hidden in the things we've been doing all along but haven't acknowledged.

Here's the truth, you weren't put on this earth to just clock in, pay bills, and call it a day. You were meant to thrive, to feel alive, and to make an impact. But how do you discover what that impact is supposed to be? Let me hit you with some tools that'll help you figure it out.

1. **Reflect on What Brings You Joy:** Purpose and passion go hand in hand, and the first step to finding them is thinking about what makes you feel alive. What are the activities that make you lose track of time? What are the things that, even when you're tired, you'd still get up and do? If it doesn't make your heart skip a beat, it's not your passion, honey bun.

2. **Look Back at Your Life's Clues:** Your life has been dropping hints about your purpose for a long time. Think back to your childhood—what did you love doing? What came naturally to you? Sometimes, our passions are hidden in the things we've been doing all along but haven't acknowledged.

1. **Identify the Problems You Want to Solve:** Purpose is often tied to how you can serve others. What issues or problems do you feel called to address? Whether it's empowering women, helping people heal from trauma, or supporting entrepreneurs in their journey—your purpose is often connected to making a difference.

2. **Follow Your Curiosity:** Passion doesn't always show up with fireworks and a neon sign. Sometimes, it whispers. What are you curious about? What subjects do you find yourself Googling at 2 a.m.? Follow that curiosity—it often leads to your passion.

ALIGNING YOUR LIFE AND CAREER WITH YOUR COL VALUES

Here's where things get real, once you discover your purpose, it's time to align your life and career with your core values. Because, let me tell you, if you're living out of alignment, you'll always feel like something's off. You could have the perfect job on paper, but if it doesn't align with who you truly are, it's going to feel like you're wearing someone else's shoes. And baby, we don't do uncomfortable shoes!

Here's how to start living in alignment with your core values:

1. **Identify Your Core Values:** First, you've got to know what those values are! Do you value freedom, creativity, connection, or making an impact? Whatever it is, get clear on what you stand for. These are your non-negotiables, the things that make you feel fulfilled.

2. **Evaluate Your Current Life:** Take a hard look at your life and career. Are they aligned with those core values? If you value creativity but your job is all about spreadsheets and data entry, we've got a problem. If you value freedom but feel trapped in your routine, it's time to make some adjustments.

3. **Make Adjustments Where Necessary:** You don't have to flip your life upside down overnight, but start making small changes that bring you closer to living in alignment. Maybe it's starting a side hustle that aligns with your passion or spending more time on activities that fulfill you. Little by little, you'll start to feel more connected to your purpose.

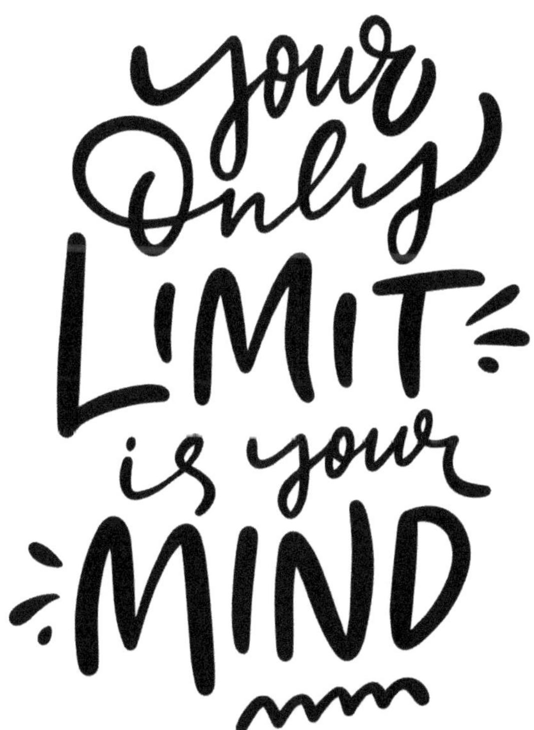

EXERCISES TO HELP YOU DISCOVER YOUR CALLIN

Let's get practical because discovering your purpose isn't just about thinking deep thoughts; it's about doing the work. Grab your journal and let's dive into some exercises to get those wheels turning.

1. **The Passion Audit:** List out everything you've ever been passionate about, from childhood until now. Don't leave anything off the list, no matter how random it seems. Now, look for patterns. What keeps popping up? What common themes do you see? This will give you a clue about what truly lights you up.

2. **The Ideal Day Visualization:** Close your eyes and imagine your ideal day, from the moment you wake up until you go to bed. What are you doing? Who are you with? How do you feel? Write down every detail. This exercise gives you insight into the kind of life you want to live—and your purpose is often tied to creating that life.

3. **The 5 Whys:** Take one of your passions or interests and ask yourself "Why?" five times. For example, if you say, "I want to start a coaching business," ask yourself why. Then keep asking why until you've dug down to the root of it. This will help you uncover your deeper motivations and purpose.

4. **The Eulogy Exercise:** I know, it sounds a little morbid, but stick with me. Imagine it's the end of your life, and people are speaking at your funeral. What do you want them to say about you? What kind of impact do you want to be remembered for? This exercise helps you focus on what really matters to you.

Wrapping It Up

Discovering your purpose and passion isn't a one-time event; it's a process. It's about being open to where life is leading you, following those little nudges from the universe, and trusting that you have something unique to offer the world.

Here's the truth, your purpose isn't hiding from you—you just have to listen, look within, and take action. When you align your life with your core values and follow your passions, everything else falls into place. So, are you ready to step into your purpose and live a life that feels deeply fulfilling? Let's get to it!

PART 3
Coach

CHAPTER 7

The Fundamentals of Coaching

life coaching

Alright, let's get real—you want to be a coach, but not just any coach. You want to be an effective, transformational coach who knows how to help people change their lives. And let me tell you, that's no small feat. But don't worry, I've got you! We're about to dive into the essentials of life coaching so you can step into your purpose with confidence and clarity.

" *Coaching is the art of unlocking potential, guiding others to see their own greatness, and empowering them to take bold steps toward their dreams.* "
-DR. TANDY

WHAT IS LIFE COACHING, AND WHAT DOES IT ENTAIL?

Let's clear something up right out of the gate, life coaching is not therapy, and it's not consulting. You're not here to fix anyone's past or tell them what to do. Nope. **Coaching is all about guiding your clients to find their own answers.** You're their guide, their cheerleader, and sometimes, the person who lovingly kicks them into gear when they're stuck.

Coaching is about creating a safe space where people can explore their dreams, confront their fears, and unlock their potential. You're there to help them see possibilities they couldn't see for themselves and hold them accountable to becoming the person they're meant to be. The magic of coaching lies in helping clients connect with their own wisdom—and that's where transformation happens.

Coaching entails:

1. **Asking the right questions:** It's not about giving advice; it's about asking powerful questions that lead your client to their own insights. You're guiding them to the breakthrough, not handing it to them.

2. **Holding space:** You've got to create an environment where your clients feel safe enough to be vulnerable and honest. They need to trust that you're fully present, non-judgmental, and there to support them 100%.

3. **Providing accountability:** People need a coach because they're ready to level up, but they need someone to help them stay on track. That's you! You're there to hold them to their word, celebrate their wins, and keep them moving forward.

THE SKILLS AND QUALITIES OF AN EFFECTIVE COACH

Now, let's talk about what it takes to be an effective coach. Not everyone is cut out for this work, but if you're reading this, you've got what it takes—you just need to sharpen those skills. Here's what separates a great coach from someone who's just playing the part:

1. **Active Listening:** I cannot stress this enough—being a great coach starts with being a great listener. And no, I'm not talking about listening so you can respond. I'm talking about deep listening—where you're fully tuned into your client's words, emotions, and the things they're not saying. When you listen deeply, you catch the cues that lead to breakthroughs.

2. **Empathy:** As a coach, you've got to meet your clients where they are. That means showing empathy for their struggles and understanding their journey. It doesn't mean you have to agree with everything they say, but it does mean you need to connect with their feelings and help them feel seen and heard.

3. **Asking Powerful Questions:** The right question at the right time can change everything. Your job is to ask questions that challenge your client's perspective, open their mind to new possibilities, and get them to dig deep. Great questions don't have yes or no answers —they make the client pause and think.

4. **Intuition:** Yes, baby—trust your gut! Coaching is both an art and a science. While you need to have structured techniques, you also need to trust your intuition. Sometimes, your gut will tell you to ask a question or explore an area that the client hasn't brought up yet. Trust it—your intuition is a powerful tool in helping your clients break through their blocks.

5. **Accountability & Support:** Effective coaches know how to strike the balance between holding their clients accountable and offering support. You're there to call them out on their excuses (with love!) while also cheering them on through the hard stuff. It's a delicate dance, but when you get it right, your clients will feel empowered to push through their fears and get results.

...DERSTANDING THE COACHING RELATIONSHIP AND SETTING BOUNDARIES

Let's talk boundaries. A lot of new coaches get tripped up here, so listen closely, **boundaries are essential in a coaching relationship.** Without clear boundaries, you'll end up burnt out, and your client won't get the best version of you.

1. **Establish Clear Roles:** Your client needs to understand what coaching is—and what it's not. You're not their therapist, their best friend, or their savior. You're their guide. Set clear expectations from the beginning about what your role is and what they can expect from the coaching process.

2. **Set Time Boundaries:** It's tempting to want to go over time when your client is in the middle of a breakthrough, but trust me—stick to your session times. It's about respecting both your time and theirs. If they need more support, schedule another session, but don't let your coaching run off the rails.

3. **Emotional Boundaries:** Coaching is emotional work, but you've got to keep clear boundaries around what you're responsible for. You are not responsible for your client's emotional well-being. You can hold space for them, but you're not there to absorb their emotions. Remember: you're a guide, not a crutch.

4. **Confidentiality:** This is non-negotiable. Your client needs to trust that what they share in a session stays in that session. Establish this up front and stick to it. This builds trust and respect in the coaching relationship.

5. **Client's Responsibility:** It's important to remind your client that they're responsible for their own results. You're there to support and guide them, but they have to put in the work. If they're not following through, that's on them—not you. Hold them accountable, but don't take on the responsibility of their success or failure.

Wrapping It Up

Coaching is one of the most rewarding careers out there because you get to witness people stepping into their power and transforming their lives. But being a coach is about more than just cheering from the sidelines—you've got to have the skills, the boundaries, and the heart to guide your clients to their breakthroughs.

If you're ready to do the work, sharpen your tools, and commit to this journey, you're going to be an unstoppable force in your clients' lives. They'll remember you not for giving them the answers, but for empowering them to find their own.

Let's get to it, coach! You've got lives to change!

CHAPTER 8
Developing Your Coaching Style

Alright, future rockstar coach, it's time to talk about something that's going to set you apart from the rest of the coaching crowd, **your unique coaching style**. This is where the magic happens, where you take everything you've learned, everything you've been through, and turn it into your secret sauce. No one can coach the way you can. Why? Because no one else has lived your journey, learned your lessons, or developed your perspective. So, let's dive into how you find your unique voice and create a coaching style that's all yours.

"Your coaching style is your unique way of empowering others—it's the blend of empathy, intuition, and strategy that helps unlock their path to success."
-DR. TANDY

DIFFERENT COACHING STYLES AND FINDING YOU[R] UNIQUE APPROACH

There are a million different ways to coach, and guess what? There's no one "right" way. Some coaches are super direct, some are nurturing, and others love to get all woo-woo and spiritual. The key to success? **You've got to be YOU.** Clients don't want a cookie-cutter coach; they want someone they connect with. Let's explore a few different coaching styles and how to figure out which one feels authentic to you.

1. **The Tough-Love Coach:** This is the coach who's not afraid to call people out on their excuses. If you're someone who thrives on accountability and pushing people out of their comfort zone, this might be your jam. You're the coach who's like, "Get up and do the work!"—but with love, of course.

2. **The Compassionate Guide:** Maybe you're more of the nurturing type. You love creating a safe space for your clients to explore their feelings and challenges. You guide them with empathy and compassion, holding space for their healing while gently encouraging them to grow.

4. **The Spiritual Guru:** If you're someone who loves to connect with energy, intuition, and all things metaphysical, this might be your lane. You might incorporate tools like meditation, visualization, or even energy healing into your coaching sessions to help your clients align with their higher selves.

5. **The Structured Strategist:** Some coaches are all about systems and strategies. You love to create clear roadmaps and action plans for your clients, helping them break down big goals into bite-sized steps. You're the coach who's all about execution and making things happen.

Here's the thing—**you don't have to pick just one style.** The best coaches are a blend of many styles. Maybe you're tough when you need to be, but you've also got a nurturing side. Or maybe you're like me—a mix of strategic thinking with a bit of woo-woo magic. Yep, woo-woo, that's my lane! I blend coaching with spiritual and intuitive practices because I know that when you align the head and the heart, that's where real transformation happens. The goal is to find the combination that feels authentic to you and resonates with your clients.

HOW TO LEVERAGE YOUR PERSONAL HEALING JOURNEY IN YOUR COACHING PRACTICE

Here's where your story becomes your superpower. Everything you've been through—the struggles, the breakthroughs, the growth—that's all part of what makes you a powerful coach. **Your healing journey is your greatest asset** because it gives you a unique perspective and the ability to deeply empathize with your clients.

So, how do you leverage that in your coaching practice? Let's break it down:

1. **Be Vulnerable:** Don't be afraid to share parts of your story with your clients. You don't have to spill all the details, but when you share the lessons you've learned from your own healing, it builds trust and connection. Your clients need to know that you've been through the fire too—and you made it out stronger.

3. **Use Your Experiences as Teaching Moments:** Think back to the turning points in your journey. What tools or mindsets helped you get through the tough times? Share those with your clients. Your personal experiences are gold mines of wisdom that can help others find their way through similar challenges.

4. **Understand What Your Clients Are Feeling**: Because you've done the healing work yourself, you can often spot when a client is stuck in a place you've been before. You understand their fear, their resistance, and their doubt because you've been there too. Use that insight to gently guide them through their own process.

5. **Lead by Example:** One of the most powerful things you can do as a coach is model what healing and growth look like. When your clients see that you're living proof of the transformation you're offering, it gives them hope. Show them what's possible by being the embodiment of your coaching principles.

BUILDING EMPATHY AND ACTIVE LISTENING SKIL

If there's one thing that separates a great coach from a mediocre one, it's **empathy**. You can have all the strategies and tools in the world, but if you can't meet your clients where they are emotionally, you're going to miss the mark. Empathy allows you to connect with your clients on a deep level, and that's where true transformation happens.

Let's talk about how to build those empathy muscles:

1. **Practice Deep Listening:** I know we've touched on this before, but it's so important, we're going to dive deeper. Active listening isn't just about hearing the words your client is saying—it's about understanding the emotions behind those words. Pay attention to their tone, their body language, and the pauses in their speech. Often, what's left unsaid is just as important as what's spoken.

2. **Put Yourself in Their Shoes**: Try to imagine what your client is feeling. If they're scared to take a big leap, think about a time when you felt the same way. When you can relate to their emotions, even if their experience is different from yours, you're better equipped to guide them through it with compassion and understanding.

3. **Reflect and Validate:** When a client shares something difficult, reflect it back to them. Say something like, "I hear that you're feeling frustrated about this situation. That makes sense, and I can see why this is hard for you." This simple act of validation can make your client feel deeply understood and supported, which builds trust and opens the door to deeper coaching.

4. **Resist the Urge to "Fix":** As coaches, we sometimes want to jump in and solve our clients' problems. But here's the thing: coaching isn't about fixing—it's about empowering. Instead of trying to offer quick solutions, let your client talk through their challenges. Your role is to guide them to their own insights, not to hand them the answers.

Wrapping It Up

Developing your coaching style is about finding your voice, leveraging your personal experiences, and building strong connections through empathy and active listening. The most powerful coaches aren't the ones with all the answers—they're the ones who know how to create a space where their clients can discover the answers for themselves.

So, what's your coaching style? How are you going to show up in a way that's authentic, impactful, and uniquely you? Remember, your story, your journey, and your heart are your greatest assets. Embrace them, hone your skills, and get ready to change some lives. You've got this!

CHAPTER 9

Building Your Coaching Practice

Alright, gorgeous souls, let's get into the juicy stuff —purpose and passion. Now, I know what you're thinking: "Dr. Tandy, how am I supposed to find my purpose when I'm just trying to make it through the day?" Well, buckle up, because we're about to dig deep and uncover what lights your soul on fire. Your purpose isn't some mystical thing hidden in a far-off place; it's inside you, and we're going to bring it out into the light.

"Building a coaching practice is about more than just offering guidance—it's about creating a space for transformation, fostering trust, and empowering others to achieve lasting change."
-DR. TANDY

STEPS TO START A COACHING BUSINESS: CERTIFICATIONS, NICHES, AND MARKETING

Starting a coaching business might feel a little overwhelming, but trust me—if I can do it, so can you. Let's break it down step-by-step so you can get started with confidence.

- **Get Certified (or Don't):** Listen, certification can be a great way to build credibility and sharpen your skills, but let me be real with you—it's not the only way. Plenty of successful coaches have built their practices without formal certification, relying on their experience, knowledge, and passion to guide them. That said, if certification feels right for you, go for it! Look for reputable programs that align with your coaching style and offer practical, hands-on learning. Whether it's through life coaching certifications or something more specific like hypnotherapy or Emotion Code (you know I'm certified in those!), make sure whatever you choose resonates with your vision.

- **Find Your Niche:** If you're trying to be everything to everyone, you'll end up being nothing to no one. Finding your niche is critical. Ask yourself: Who do I feel called to serve? Is it people struggling with confidence, relationships, career transitions? Get specific. Your niche isn't just about who you serve but also about how you serve them. Are you the no-nonsense coach? The spiritual, woo-woo guide? The tough-love truth-teller? Own your lane, and don't be afraid to carve out a space that's all yours.

- **Get Visible (Marketing 101):** You can be the best coach in the world, but if nobody knows about you, you're not going to be able to change lives (or make a living). Marketing is all about showing up, being consistent, and putting yourself out there. Start with a website, get on social media, and create content that speaks to your ideal clients. Don't be shy—share your story, share your expertise, and let people know how you can help them transform. I know marketing can feel intimidating, but remember, you're not selling—you're serving. People need what you have to offer, so let them know how to find you.

ETHICAL CONSIDERATIONS AND MAINTAINING PROFESSIONAL STANDARDS

Now, let's talk about something that can get overlooked but is absolutely non-negotiable: ethics and professionalism. As a coach, you're not just a business owner—you're in a position of trust, and that comes with serious responsibility.

- **Confidentiality:** This is rule number one, and it should go without saying. What happens in a coaching session stays in the coaching session. Your clients need to feel safe sharing their deepest fears, struggles, and dreams with you. If they can't trust you, they won't open up, and if they don't open up, you can't help them.
- **Clear Boundaries:** Remember, you're a coach—not a therapist, not a friend, and not a business partner. It's so important to keep the relationship professional while still being compassionate and empathetic. Set clear boundaries with your clients about what's okay and what's not. This could be around session times, communication outside of sessions, or expectations for progress.

- **Stay in Your Lane:** As much as you might want to, you're not equipped to help every single person in every single way. If a client's issues go beyond your expertise—like serious mental health concerns—it's crucial to refer them to a licensed professional. Know your limits, and don't try to be all things to all people.

- **Keep Learning:** The best coaches are lifelong learners. Just because you've started your practice doesn't mean the learning stops. Stay up to date on new coaching techniques, attend workshops, get supervision, and always be looking for ways to improve your skills. The more you grow, the more you can help your clients grow.

BUILDING A BRAND AND ATTRACTING CLIENTS

Let's talk branding, baby! Your brand is more than just your logo or your website—it's the essence of who you are and what you stand for. It's how you make people feel when they come into contact with you, whether that's through your website, your social media, or in person. So, how do you build a brand that attracts clients who are ready to do the work?

- **Know Your Vibe:** Your brand should reflect **you.** Are you the calm, grounded coach who helps people find their inner peace, or are you the energetic, no-BS coach who pushes people out of their comfort zones? Whatever your style, make sure your branding reflects it. From your colors to your messaging, everything should feel aligned with who you are as a coach. I'm all about that mix of **woo-woo magic** and real-life strategy, and everything I put out reflects that vibe. Find yours and rock it.

- **Create Value:** Attracting clients isn't just about posting pretty pictures on Instagram. You need to create content that **adds value** to people's lives. Think blog posts, videos, free workshops, or social media posts that give your audience a taste of what you can help them with. When you show up with solutions to their problems, they'll start to see you as the go-to person for the help they need.

- **Build Relationships:** People hire coaches they trust, and that trust is built through relationships. Engage with your audience. Respond to comments, send DMs, and have real conversations. The more people feel connected to you, the more likely they are to work with you when they're ready to invest in themselves.
- **Stay Consistent:** Consistency is key. Whether you're sending out a weekly email, posting daily on social media, or doing monthly webinars, stick to a schedule. Show up consistently, and people will come to expect you in their lives. And when they're ready to take the leap, guess who they'll turn to? **You.**

Wrapping It Up

Building a coaching practice takes effort, dedication, and heart—but if you're in this game, I already know you've got all of that in spades. Remember, the best coaches aren't just skilled at helping others—they're also skilled at building a business that allows them to live their purpose.

So, whether you're just getting started or looking to take your practice to the next level, trust that you've got what it takes to create a coaching business that's aligned with who you are and the impact you want to make. Keep your ethics in check, find your niche, build your brand, and get out there to serve the clients who need exactly what you've got to offer. Now go build that business, coach! The world is waiting for you!

CHAPTER 10

The Business Side of Coaching

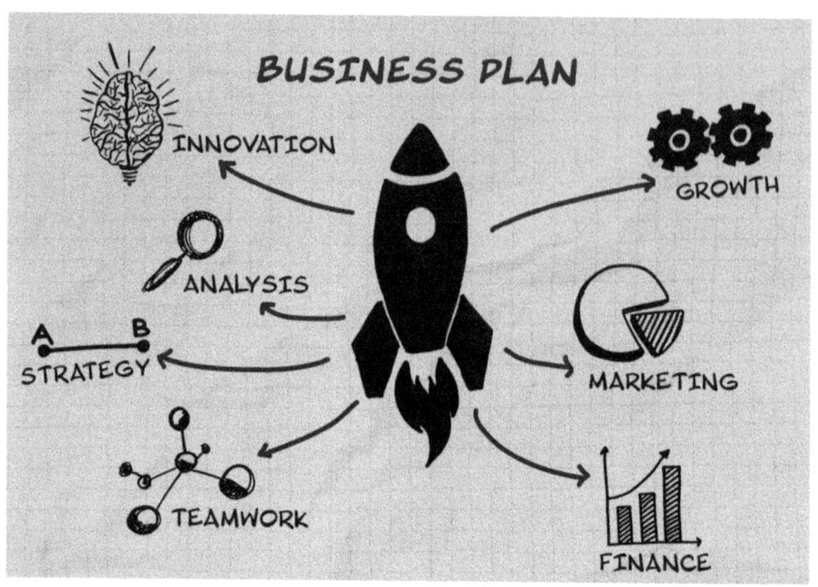

Alright, coach—now that we've laid the groundwork for your coaching magic, it's time to talk about the part that makes some people squirm: the business side of coaching. I know, I know—numbers, legal structures, and marketing might not feel as inspiring as changing lives, but let me tell you, getting this side locked down is what's going to allow you to keep doing the work you love, sustainably and profitably. If you want to build a business that thrives, you've got to get serious about the logistics. So, let's break it down and get you set up for long-term success!

"The business side of coaching is where purpose meets strategy. It's about building a sustainable foundation that allows you to serve others while growing your own impact and success."
-DR. TANDY

ETTING UP YOUR BUSINESS: LEGAL STRUCTURES, PRICING, AND SERVICES

Let's start with the basics. Before you jump in and start coaching the masses, you need to make sure your business is legit. That means thinking about legal structures, how to price your services, and what exactly you're offering.

1. Choose Your Legal Structure: Okay, first things first—you've got to set up the legal side of your business. Are you going to be a sole proprietor, an LLC (Limited Liability Company), or maybe even an S-Corp? For most new coaches, an LLC is a good middle ground. It gives you protection (because you don't want someone coming after your personal assets if something goes wrong), but it's also simple to set up and manage. Check your local regulations, and if you're not sure, consult with a small business attorney or accountant to figure out what's best for you.

2. Set Your Pricing: Oh, the dreaded pricing conversation! Let me tell you something—you are worth it. Don't undervalue yourself because you're new, or you're afraid people won't pay. You're offering a transformation, not just your time, and that's priceless. Do your research. See what other coaches in your niche are charging, and set your rates accordingly. If you're just starting out, you might offer a few beta sessions or introductory rates, but don't stay there forever. When you're good at what you do, people will pay for it.

3. Define Your Services: You need to get crystal clear on what you're offering. Are you doing one-on-one coaching, group programs, workshops, or online courses? What's the duration of your sessions, and what's included in your packages? Your services should be aligned with your strengths and the needs of your clients. Make it easy for people to understand what they're getting when they work with you. Remember, clarity attracts clients—confusion repels them.

MARKETING STRATEGIES TO GROW YOUR CLIENT BASE

Now that your business is set up, let's talk about how to get those clients rolling in! Marketing might sound like a scary word, but really, it's just about showing up and letting people know how you can help them. It's about building trust, offering value, and positioning yourself as the go-to coach in your niche.

1. **Know Your Audience:** You've got to know **who** you're speaking to. What are their struggles, their goals, their desires? When you can articulate your ideal client's pain points better than they can, they're going to feel seen and understood—and they'll know you're the coach for them. So, get clear on who your ideal client is and what they need.

2. **Create Valuable Content:** People need to see you, hear from you, and learn from you before they'll hire you. That's where content comes in. Whether it's blog posts, podcasts, YouTube videos, or Instagram lives, you've got to be out there sharing your wisdom and expertise. Don't be afraid to give away valuable content—because when people see the free stuff you're offering, they'll wonder, "If this is the free content, imagine what I'll get when I hire them!"

3. **Leverage Social Proof:** Nothing speaks louder than results. As you work with clients, collect testimonials and case studies that show how your coaching has helped people transform. Put these front and center on your website and social media. Potential clients want to know that you can get results, and nothing convinces them more than seeing others who have already walked that path with you.

4. **Network and Collaborate:** Sometimes the best way to grow your business is by partnering with others. Find people who serve a similar audience and collaborate on workshops, webinars, or live events. Networking with other professionals in your space helps expand your reach and brings you, new clients, from people who trust their recommendations.

MANAGING FINANCES AND SUSTAINING YOUR PRACTICE

Let's talk money, honey! Coaching is a business, and like any business, you've got to be smart with your finances if you want to keep the doors open and the lights on. Here's how you manage your money like a boss and ensure your practice is sustainable for the long haul.

1.   **Track Your Income and Expenses:** It might not be glamorous, but you need to know where your money is going. Keep track of every dollar that comes in and goes out. There are tons of software options out there, like QuickBooks or FreshBooks, that make this easy. Make sure you're setting aside enough for taxes (trust me, you don't want a surprise bill from Uncle Sam at the end of the year), and keep your business and personal expenses separate.

2. **Set Up Multiple Streams of Income:** One-on-one coaching is amazing, but let's be real—it's not always scalable. You can only coach so many people in a day. That's why it's smart to build multiple streams of income. Think about offering group programs, creating digital products like eBooks or courses, or hosting paid workshops. This way, you're not relying on just one source of revenue.

4. **Save for Slow Seasons:** Business ebbs and flows, and coaching is no different. There will be months when clients are lining up, and there may be slow seasons. Plan for it. Make sure you're setting aside some of your income during the busy times to cover the slower months. This will give you peace of mind and keep your stress levels in check when things aren't as busy.

5. **Invest in Yourself and Your Business**: You are your greatest asset. As a coach, you need to keep growing and evolving if you want your business to thrive. Invest in your own development—whether it's through hiring your own coach, attending workshops, or taking courses. The more you invest in yourself, the more value you bring to your clients, and that keeps them coming back.

Wrapping It Up

Look, I know the business side of coaching might not feel as fun as the actual coaching, but it's essential if you want to build something that lasts. You've got to set up your business right, market yourself consistently, and be smart about your money. When you've got these pieces in place, not only will your coaching practice thrive, but you'll also have the freedom and flexibility to live the life you've always wanted.

So go out there and build your empire! You're not just a coach—you're a business owner, a leader, and a game-changer. And trust me, when you get your business in order, you'll be unstoppable. Let's get it, coach!

Final Thoughts

YOUR ONGOING JOURNEY

Alright, my beautiful souls, let's bring it all together. If you've made it this far, you're not just interested in becoming a coach—you're ready to transform lives, starting with your own. But here's the truth: this journey you're on? It doesn't have an endpoint. **Coaching is a lifelong commitment to growth, healing, and leveling up,** not just for your clients but for yourself. So let's talk about how to keep that momentum going, how to protect your energy, and how to step into your purpose with confidence.

"Ongoing journeys remind us that growth is a process, not a destination. Every step forward deepens our wisdom and expands our capacity to become who we're meant to be."
-DR. TANDY

EMBRACING CONTINUOUS GROWTH AS A COACH AND INDIVIDUAL

Here's the thing about being a coach, you've got to **keep evolving.** You can't help others grow if you're stagnant in your own life. This is an ongoing journey of learning, unlearning, and relearning. Every new client will teach you something. Every challenge you face will sharpen your skills. The more you grow as an individual, the more impactful you'll be as a coach.

So how do you keep growing? Stay curious. Seek out new experiences. Read the books, take the courses, attend the workshops. Don't be afraid to get coached yourself! The best coaches are the ones who know what it's like to be in the client's shoes—who understand the vulnerability of asking for help and the power of receiving it.

Never get too comfortable, honey. **Comfort is the enemy of growth.** The more you push your boundaries, the more expansive your life—and your coaching practice—will become.

THE IMPORTANCE OF SELF-CARE AND AVOIDING BURNOUT

Now, let's get real about something a lot of coaches don't talk about enough **self-care.** You can't pour from an empty cup. If you're not taking care of yourself, you're not going to be able to show up fully for your clients, your business, or your life. Burnout is real, and trust me, it will sneak up on you if you're not mindful of your energy.

Here's what I want you to remember: **you are your first client.** That means you need to make your mental, emotional, and physical well-being a priority. Set boundaries with your clients and yourself. Take breaks when you need them. Unplug. Say no to things that drain your energy and yes to things that restore it.

Self-care isn't a luxury—it's a necessity. Whether that looks like daily meditation, spending time in nature, or just saying "no" without feeling guilty, you've got to build practices that keep you grounded and refreshed. Because when you take care of you, you show up as the most powerful, vibrant version of yourself—and that's the coach your clients need.

TAKING YOUR FIRST STEP TOWARDS HEALING, GROWTH, AND COACHING

If you're still reading this, then you already know—you're meant for more. You're meant to heal, grow, and step into your role as a coach who changes lives. But here's the thing: none of this happens if you don't take that **first step.**

It doesn't matter if you're scared. It doesn't matter if you don't feel ready. You don't need to have everything figured out before you start. The only thing you need is the courage to take action—one small step in the direction of your dreams. And if you already have that first step, maybe it's time to work with **Dr. Tandy** to push you even further, to deepen your transformation, and bring your coaching vision to life.

Whether your next move is working on your own healing, getting certified, or putting yourself out there to attract clients, **do something today** that moves you closer to your goal. You don't have to have all the answers—you just have to be willing to take the leap. And if you're ready for that next level, working with me is where we make those breakthroughs happen. You don't have to do it alone—I'm here to guide you.

Because here's what I know for sure, **you are ready**. You've been through the fire, you've done the work, and now it's time to help others do the same. The world needs your gifts, your wisdom, and your light. So don't wait—step into your power, own your story, and start this beautiful journey of healing, growth, and coaching.

I believe in you. Now it's time for you to believe in yourself. Whether you're starting or leveling up with me, let's go get it, coach! The world is waiting.

APPENDICES

RECOMMENDED BOOKS, RESOURCES, AND TOOLS FOR HEALING AND COACHING

Here's a list of books, resources, and tools that I personally recommend for deepening your healing journey and sharpening your coaching skills. Whether you're just starting out or looking to take your practice to the next level, these will support you in your growth.

Books for Coaching:

- **The Coaching Habit by Michael Bungay Stanier** — A practical guide to becoming a better coach by asking the right questions.
- **Co-Active Coaching by Henry Kimsey-House** — A foundational book that covers the basics of powerful, transformational coaching.
- **The Prosperous Coach by Steve Chandler and Rich Litvin** — A must-read for any coach looking to build a thriving coaching business.
- **Dare to Lead by Brené Brown** — A book on courage and leadership, perfect for coaches who want to empower others.

Books for Healing:

- **Boundaries + Clarity = Peace by Dr. Tandy —** Learn how setting clear boundaries brings you peace and freedom in life and relationships.
- **The Diva Code by Dr. Tandy —** Unlock your inner confidence and embrace your true self with this empowering guide for every woman ready to step into her power.
- **Forgiveness is Therapeutic by Dr. Tandy —** A powerful resource for those ready to release resentment and embrace the healing power of forgiveness.
- **Date Thyself by Dr. Tandy —** A guide to breaking the cycle of toxic relationships by nurturing your relationship with yourself and changing your energy signature.
- **The Body Keeps the Score by Bessel van der Kolk —** A deep dive into how trauma affects the body and mind, and how to heal from it.
- **The Emotion Code by Dr. Bradley Nelson —** Learn how to release trapped emotions for emotional freedom.
- **You Can Heal Your Life by Louise Hay —** A classic in the world of self-healing, focusing on affirmations and mindset shifts.

Tools and Resources:

- **Journaling:** Whether you're healing or coaching, journaling is a powerful tool for reflection and growth. Tools like The Five Minute Journal or guided journaling apps can be useful.
- **Meditation Apps:** Headspace and Insight Timer are great for practicing mindfulness and grounding yourself before sessions.
- **Coaching Tools**: Use platforms like Zoom for virtual coaching, Acuity for scheduling, and Kajabi for creating and selling digital courses or coaching programs.

These resources will support your journey of healing and growth as you step into your role as a transformational coach!

SAMPLE COACHING SESSION OUTLINE AND QUESTIONS

Here's a sample framework to guide your coaching sessions. Remember, your style is unique, but having a structure helps you stay focused and provide value in every session.

Coaching Session Outline:

1. **Check-In (5-10 minutes):**
   - Start by asking your client how they've been feeling since the last session.
   - What progress have they made? What challenges did they face?

Sample Question: "What's been the most significant thing you've learned about yourself since our last session?"

2. **Session Focus (5 minutes):**
   - Identify the focus for this session. Ask your client what they want to work on today.
   - Set an intention for the session.

Sample Question: "What's the biggest challenge or goal on your mind today that you'd like to work through?"

3. **Exploration and Discovery (20-25 minutes):**
- Dive deep into the issue or goal your client has brought up.
- Use open-ended questions to guide them to their own insights and breakthroughs.

Sample Questions:

- "What's behind this challenge for you?"
- "How does this situation make you feel, and why?"
- "What's stopping you from moving forward?"

4. **Action Planning (10-15 minutes):**
- Help your client create a plan for taking action based on the insights gained during the session.
- Make sure the action steps are specific and achievable.

Sample Questions:

- "What's one action you can take this week to move closer to your goal?"
- "What support do you need to make this happen?"

5. **Closing and Reflection (5 minutes):**

- End the session with a reflection on the progress made and a recap of the action plan.
- Offer encouragement and set a date for the next session.

Sample Question: "What's your biggest takeaway from today's session, and how are you feeling about the steps we've outlined?"

SELF-ASSESSMENT TOOLS FOR POTENTIAL COACHES

Before stepping into your role as a coach, it's essential to do some self-reflection. These self-assessment tools will help you evaluate your readiness, identify your strengths, and discover areas where you can grow.

1. Core Strengths as a Coach:

Rate yourself on a scale of 1-10 in the following areas:

- Active Listening
- Empathy
- Asking Powerful Questions
- Accountability
- Emotional Intelligence

Reflection: Which areas do you feel most confident in? Which areas do you need to develop further?

2. Passion and Purpose Alignment:

- What excites you most about becoming a coach?
- Who do you feel called to help, and why?
- How does coaching align with your core values and life purpose?

3. Emotional Resilience:

- Think back to a time when you faced a major challenge. How did you handle it?
- Are you able to separate your emotions from your clients' emotions during a session?
- What are your strategies for managing stress and avoiding burnout?

4. Business Mindset:

- Are you comfortable with promoting yourself and your services?
- How do you feel about setting pricing and charging clients for your time and expertise?
- What's your vision for your coaching business in the next 1-3 years?

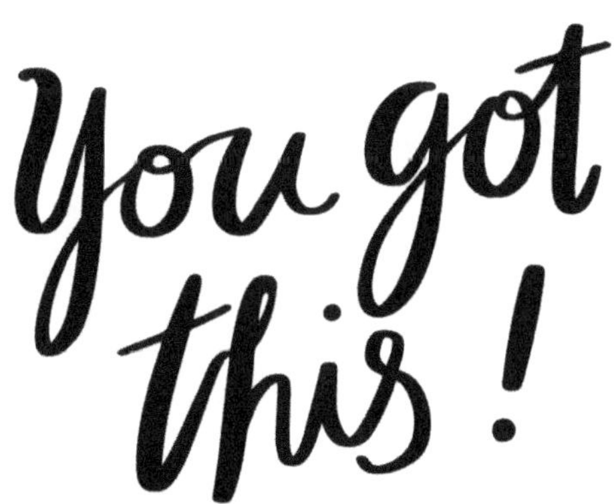

5. Commitment to Growth:

- How committed are you to your own personal development as a coach?
- What ongoing learning or certifications are you interested in pursuing?
- How do you plan to stay accountable to your growth and your clients' success?

These tools, resources, and exercises are designed to help you step into your role as a coach with confidence and clarity. Remember, being a great coach starts with working on yourself first, so don't skip this part of the process!

STAY COMMITED!

21
Day Journal To
Unlock Your Potential

" *Journaling is a conversation with your soul—a space where clarity, healing, and self-discovery unfold.*"

-DR.TANDY

Welcome to your 21-Day Journal To Unlock Your Potential

This journey is an opportunity for you to dive deep into your thoughts, emotions, and experiences, fostering a greater understanding of yourself, and laying the foundation for your growth as a coach. Becoming a coach isn't just about helping others; it's about understanding your own inner world first. This self-awareness empowers you to guide others more effectively, with empathy and authenticity.

Reflection is one of the most powerful tools in a coach's toolkit. It allows you to pause, look inward, and explore the nuances of your own experiences. By engaging in daily reflection, you can uncover insights that will shape not only your coaching practice but also your life, providing clarity, purpose, and a deepened sense of self.

Over the next 21 days, you will be guided through a series of prompts designed to help you navigate the core aspects of becoming a coach—understanding your own journey, honing key skills, and preparing to serve others. Each prompt encourages honest introspection and challenges you to confront the thoughts, emotions, and experiences that will inform your future coaching style.

Why 21 Days?

Research suggests it takes approximately 21 days to form a new habit. By committing to this journal for the next three weeks, you are cultivating a lasting habit of reflection and self-exploration. This practice is essential in becoming an effective coach, as it trains you to look beyond the surface and develop the deeper insight necessary to guide others.

What to Expect

Each day, you'll be presented with a prompt or activity designed to help you explore different aspects of your development as a coach. Some prompts will focus on understanding your personal growth and how it relates to your coaching journey, while others may challenge you to explore coaching-specific skills, like listening, empathy, and questioning techniques.

How to Use This Journal

Create a Dedicated Space: Find a quiet, comfortable space where you can write without interruptions. This will be your sanctuary for reflection.

1. Set Aside Time: Dedicate a specific time each day for journaling. Consistency is key to forming a new habit and making the most of this experience.

2. Be Honest: Approach each prompt with an open mind and heart. Honest reflection is where true growth begins.

3. Take Your Time: There is no rush. Allow yourself the freedom to write as much or as little as you need. Some prompts may require more time and thought, and that's perfectly okay.

4. Revisit and Reflect: Periodically look back on your entries to see how your thoughts and feelings have evolved. This can provide valuable insights and reinforce your progress.

The Power of Reflection in Coaching

As a coach, one of the greatest gifts you can offer your clients is the ability to truly listen and guide them in reflecting on their own lives. But before you can do that effectively, you must develop that skill within yourself. This 21-day journey will teach you how to listen to your inner voice, validate your emotions, and recognize your own patterns, preparing you to help others do the same.

Through reflection, you'll uncover the roots of your own motivations, identify areas for growth, and set goals that will shape your path as a coach. By the end of these 21 days, you will not only have deepened your understanding of yourself but also sharpened the tools and skills essential to being a transformative coach.

As you embark on this journey, be patient and kind to yourself. Self-discovery takes time, and reflection may bring up emotions or insights you hadn't expected. Embrace the process, knowing that it will lead you to become the coach you aspire to be.

Welcome to your 21-day journey of growth and transformation. Take a deep breath, open your mind, and begin.

Setting Intentions

Why do you want to become a coach? What impact
do you hope to have on others?

Activity: Write a mission statement for your
coaching practice.

Discovering Your Strengths

What are your top three strengths that you can bring to your coaching practice?

Activity: Reflect on a time when you used these strengths effectively.

Identifying Areas for Growth

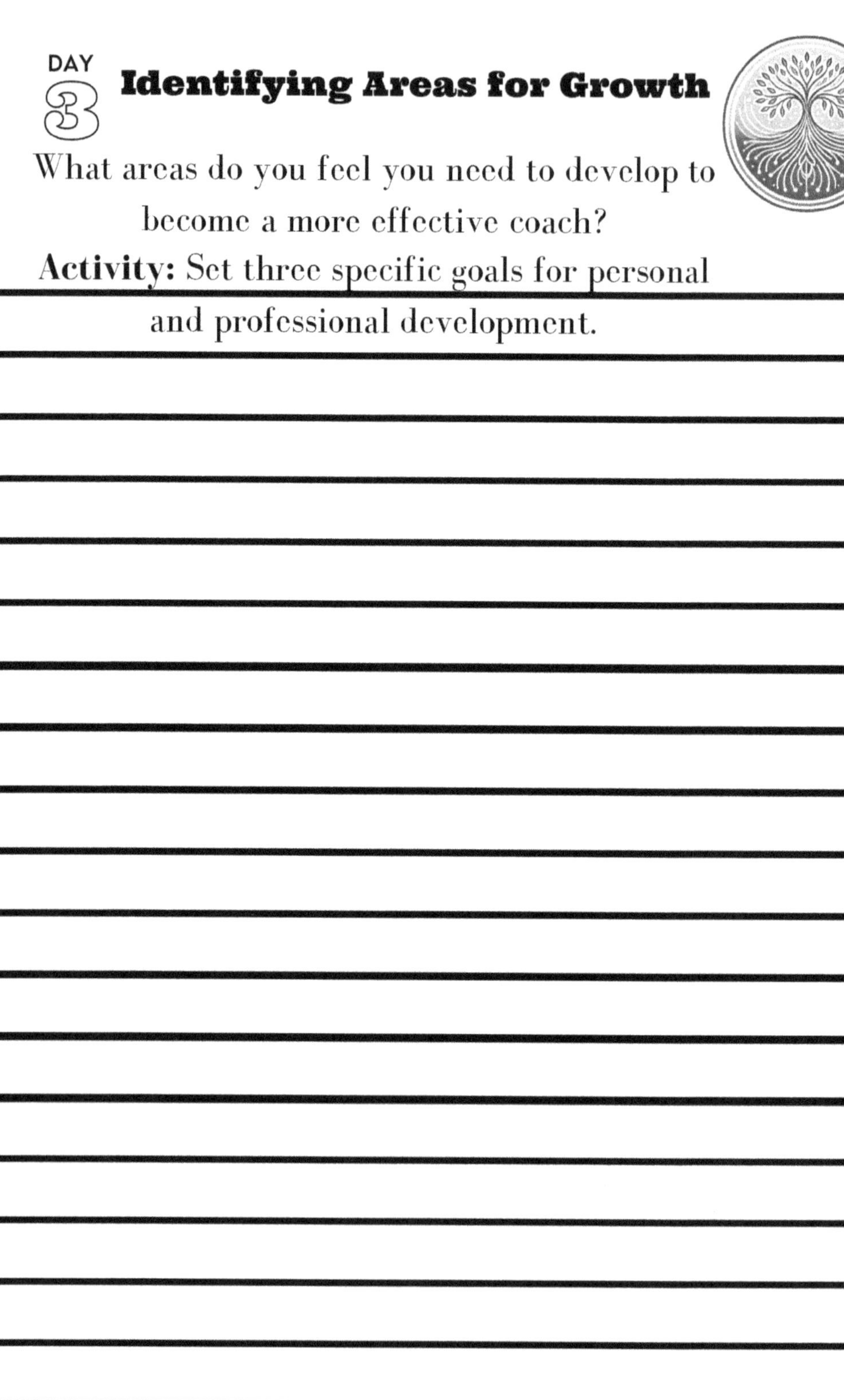

What areas do you feel you need to develop to become a more effective coach?

Activity: Set three specific goals for personal and professional development.

Understanding Your Coaching Style

What is your unique coaching style? Are you more of
a motivator, a strategist, or a listener?
Activity: Write about a time when you helped
someone using this style.

Creating a Safe Space
for Clients

How will you create a safe and supportive
environment for your clients?

Activity: List five ways to ensure confidentiality and
build trust.

Developing Active Listening Skills

Why is active listening important in coaching?

Activity: Practice active listening with a friend or colleague and reflect on the experience.

The Power of Open-Ended Questions

How can open-ended questions facilitate deeper conversations?

Activity: Write down five open-ended questions you could use in a coaching session.

Building Empathy and Understanding

How can you cultivate empathy in your coaching practice?

Activity: Reflect on a time when you felt deeply understood and how that experience impacted you.

Navigating Difficult Conversations

What strategies can you use to handle difficult conversations with clients?

Activity: Write a script for a challenging coaching scenario and how you would navigate it.

Setting Boundaries and Managing Expectations

Why is it important to set boundaries with your clients?

Activity: Define your boundaries and write them down clearly.

Cultivating Self-Awareness

How can increasing your self-awareness benefit your coaching practice?

Activity: Spend 10 minutes in meditation or quiet reflection, focusing on your inner state.

Embracing Feedback

How do you respond to feedback, and how can you use it to improve?

Activity: Seek feedback from a peer or mentor and write about what you learned.

The Art of Goal Setting

Why is goal-setting important in coaching?

Activity: Outline a SMART goal framework for a hypothetical client.

Motivation and Accountability

How will you keep yourself and your clients
motivated and accountable?

Activity: Create a plan for tracking progress and
celebrating wins.

Developing Your Coaching Toolkit

What tools and techniques will you use in your coaching sessions?

Activity: Research and choose three coaching tools you'd like to incorporate.

Understanding the Coaching Process

What are the key phases of the coaching process?

Activity: Write out the steps you will take in a typical coaching session.

Managing Your Energy

How do you plan to manage your energy and
avoid burnout as a coach?

Activity: List three self-care practices you will
commit to.

Reflecting on Your Journey So Far

What have you learned about yourself and your
coaching aspirations in the past 17 days?
Activity: Write a letter to yourself summarizing
your journey and any new insights.

Visualizing Success

What does success look like for you as a coach?

Activity: Create a vision board or write a detailed visualization of your successful coaching practice.

Building Your Coaching Brand

How will you differentiate yourself in the coaching industry?

Activity: Draft an elevator pitch for your coaching services.

Committing to Continuous Growth

How will you continue to grow and develop as a coach?

Activity: Write a commitment statement outlining your plan for continuous learning and development.